Dear Courtney,
Thanks for your friendship
and for being a great
Publisher!

Boy
with a
Halo
at the
Farmer's
Market

SONIA GREENFIELD

Sonia ♡

Codhill Press
New Paltz, New York

CODHILL

Codhill books are published by David Appelbaum for Codhill Press

Grateful acknowledgement is made to the editors of the following publications, in which versions of some of these poems first appeared:

14 Hills: "Bodies of Water," "Body of Water"

Antioch Review: "Passing the Barnyard Graveyard"

Borderlands: "In Between Rest Stops"

Burnside Review: "Boy with a Halo at the Farmer's Market,"
"Recipe for an Old Fashioned"

Cimarron Review: "Rock Tumbler"

Cream City Review: "*Washing the Saucepans*"

Folio: "Before the Flood" (as "Flood Plain")

Green Mountains Review: "Circus Gravitas," "*Cricket Chirping in a Scarecrow's Belly*"

LUMINA: "Milk Carton Kids"

Main Street Rag: "Census," "Recipe for a Sidecar"

Massachusetts Review: "victory"

Meridian: "I Shouldn't Even Write This," "Winter Distances"

Ragazine: "An Oral History of Bodie, California," "School Rules"

Rattle: "Corpse Flower," "Sago Mine, West Virginia,"
"A Spokesperson Said Thoughts and Prayers Go Out"

Red Rock Review: "Housekeeping," "Mobile Homes"

Sow's Ear: "Correct Me," "Roadside, Railside Diner"

Sycamore Review: "In Discovery Park"

"Passing the Barnyard Graveyard" appeared in *2010 Best American Poetry*.

Some poems appeared in limited-edition chapbook *Circus Gravitas*
(Finishing Line Press, 2014).

To the clever friends who have tinkered with this manuscript on my behalf—
James Arthur, John Barrios, Megan Breiseth, Amy Gerstler, Carmen Giménez Smith,
and Megan Snyder-Camp—I thank you.

Book and cover design by Alicia Fox

Library of Congress Cataloging-in-Publication Data

Greenfield, Sonia, 1970–
[Poems. Selections]
Boy with a halo at the farmer's market / Sonia Greenfield. — First edition.
pages cm
ISBN 1-930337-83-3 (alk. paper)
I. Title.

PS3607.R4545A6 2015
811'.6—dc23

2015008486

For My Boys

CONTENTS

I

Milk Carton Kids   5
Mobile Homes   6
Nafsicrate Considers Bruegel's Famous Work   7
Body of Water   8
Pestilence   9
The Hanging Tree   10
Rock Tumbler   11
How Many Angels Can Dance on the Head of a Pin?   12
Vitreous Spirits   13
Housekeeping   14
Washing the Saucepans   15
Conquistadors   16
Afternoon with Redón   17
Riding the Ranch Roads   18
Roadside, Railside Diner   19
Circus Gravitas   20
The Hobbyist   21
Caught   22

II

Between Rest Stops   25
The Lost Boys   26
An Oral History of Bodie, California   27
Sago Mine, West Virginia   28
Cricket Chirping in a Scarecrow's Body   29
Recipe for an Old Fashioned   30
Recipe for a Sidecar   31
Celebrity Stalking   32
Killing Time in the Green Room   33
A Spokesperson Said Thoughts and Prayers Go Out   34
I Shouldn't Even Write This   35
Corpse Flower   36
Suckling   37
Henry Ford Hospital, 1932   38
Playa de los Muertos   39

III

victory   43

Many Chambered   44

Before the Flood   45

Submersed   46

Boy with a Halo at the Farmer's Market   47

Bodies of Water   48

Morning Coffee with Chagall   49

Census   50

Lost in Winter, Revised   51

Winter Distances   52

In Discovery Park   53

School Rules   54

Kicked Around   55

Correct Me   56

Twice-Missed Carriage   57

The Emperor   58

A Vision in Stride Rite   59

Passing the Barnyard Graveyard   60

About the Author   63

Boy with a Halo at the Farmer's Market

I

Everything is ceremony in the wild garden of childhood.

—PABLO NERUDA

Milk Carton Kids

Now you know they were abducted
on the way to school, past chain-link
urban puzzles, robins scrabbling in the median,
book bags hanging with the weight of history,
or off the side of a rural road in late spring
where slapped mosquitos left smears of horse blood
and the churn of a distant John Deere sounded
like the log-sawing of sleep. Or the teens taken
under the lantern of the supermoon,
by the unused railroad tracks, where flowering
quince unfolds pale pink among
the blackberry brambles and wharf rats
run the length of cool steel in search
of dropped chips. Or in the desert when dusk
slips on her silk nightie, and the saucers
scream like gulls while the aliens shape their ecto
like cacti, go green and prickly. The extra-
terrestrials tap their feet to snap on
high-beams, but we call them stars. Up the kids go
as your radio loses its tune, the television
becomes a box of static, and the digital clock
blinks five again and again. Not stuffed
in a trunk, not dragged from a lake.

Mobile Homes

The heat was in the quarry warming rocks. How long
could I break them looking for gold? All summer
long I rode circles around the trailer park

listening to popsicle sticks stutter against my spokes.
Where the road ended, a snake dried on the pavement.
The snake ended where the woods began. In the woods,

a man ate children. Beware. My collection of caterpillars
wormed their way out of my heart. When darkness cooled
our metal houses, bats hovered like an undulant ceiling.

Moths brushed their wings against my face. What spooks
a man to drink again? Pop went quiet and suspicion
crackled before the downpour. My grandmother

drew her face in. It was a season to tip a glass up.
He put a ship's bell on the side of the trailer
and rang for me across the park. I heard a bell tolling.

Nafsicrate Considers Bruegel's Famous Work

I told Daedalus to watch him, goddammit,
so now here I am waiting for my son
to breaststroke home to me, held up on fingers
of green foam. Waiting past the rise and fall
of Rome through to Pieter's brushwork
which rendered the sun like a lemon on fire,
some stupid plowman hogging the canvas,
the plunge just a few flicks of horsehair
in ochre. I have waited until the ship's sails
became rags, until metal replaced wood,
motors replaced oars. I said *you can't trust children*
to make good choices, so watch him. Do you see
how Pieter painted the toes pointed to the sky?
I taught my boy how to dive like that. Every
summer day until his teeth were chattering
and lips tinged purple, he learned crawl and kick.
Trembling over the water like a bent marigold,
he learned how to tip into the cold tarn,
hands in prayer and head first, my minnow
cutting again and again through the blue.
Let the seas dry to muddy puddles. Let
the wheat fields go to dirt. My God,
what's a mother to do? I'm leaving on
my porch light. I expect Icarus home soon.

Body of Water

Begin with a raft, which floats in the middle of a lake surrounded
by long grasses. Introduce my grandmother calling for us from shore.
Explain how she looked like a white flame against the dark trees.
Say: the fireflies were already shining. Describe how David and I
began swimming back to shore. Hint at fatigue. Develop my character
by explaining how I swam with David on my back. Then say: I kept
going under and told him he would need to swim for himself. Try
to reconstruct the sensation of almost drowning. For example, convey
the image of a young girl, around ten, in a panic, swallowing water.
Depict the realization, after reaching shore, that David was no longer
behind me. Articulate fear. For instance, mention how I vomited,
my grandmother shaking all over. Attempt a building up of despair.
Definitely recount the arrival of men with lights, which they used
to illuminate the sides of the lake. Try to make time and the sequencing
of events extend to represent the sensation of how each was distorted
by the anticipation of tragedy. Without being obvious, or melodramatic,
make it clear that my brother drowned. Say: I am afraid of water.

Pestilence

Everything went south
on Smith Street

like some hell mouth yawned
in the same cellar

where a rust clot
stained the foundation.

At night bugs came out
and flicked their shells open

like switchblades.
Our calico stashed

her stillborns
in the back of my closet.

Then the heat came
and the gypsy moths

ate everything. A cloud
of gnats blurred

the backyard shed,
fireflies illumined

the lawn into a
necromagical carpet

outside the funeral parlor
next door where

my first love lay pricked
by the roses I tucked

into his hands.
No wonder I went light

as a feather, stiff
as a board.

The Hanging Tree

The angle of shadow from the school roof,
sun backlit, and his head was a small
bubble breaking the clean line of building's edge.
Malice fell open like a dirty magazine
and he thumbed through it. The tree is in a panic
and wrings its leaves. The flag snaps, its rope
rings the pole. His brother whipped him bruises
like a vitamin deficiency. His brother beat him
like a wife. What girl could love the humiliated?
She shuffles the leaves, her chin tucked in shame.
This is no joke. A boy walks into the park, finds
the pines wanting, and decides to hang around.

Rock Tumbler

Mr. Saperstein kept animal parts
in jars along the wall, milk-eyed
in formaldehyde, kept his students
in line with cruelty, and it was the year
the boys kissed the girls while I learned
to vanish or get beat, the year
I carried stew to my stepfather
at the printing press, before he took
a hammer to our ceramic pig in overalls
and stole his kids' money to buy ruin
dressed as a stiff drink, the year
I sold my toys to the janitor
to buy make-up, and when he touched me
I turned away. It was the year I just wanted
it all back but the whirligigs stood still
when spring gave way. Our science teacher
kept a rock-tumbler at the back
of the classroom. It was the year
we'd bring in jagged stones
and he'd put them in the machine.
What he pulled out later were still rocks,
though round and perfect,
offered up to us with a slick
semiprecious gleam.

How Many Angels Can Dance on the Head of a Pin?

When I was a girl it was
six like sugar crystals
on a flat silver disc three
couples clasped with wings
folded in slow pirouettes
a tiny minuet I spied
with my magnifier for
buttercups and beetles later
turned burning lens: the sun
pulled to a hot arrow
aimed at the seraphim.

Vitreous Spirits

Blue sheep ran against
a Florida sky

when I saw floaters
in the corners of my eye.

Heat raked dry fingers
through the grass, insects buzzed

in the rag-tag yard,
thunder rolled in

like a stampede split
from the hot slash. My lambs

moved in time
with the swing-set, squeak

of chain, diamond-link fence,
mowers mowing.

Finally blessed
in the long drone of summer,

not alone, my bairn-heart
bleating.

Housekeeping

My grandmother washes paper birthday plates
and mice leave scat on her kitchen table.

Each hour, the Elvis clock croons. The television
re-runs. Plaster drifts down from the ceiling

and the bones of the house are revealed. My mother
keeps a path clear around her bed as the pillars

of mail grow up the wall, as if they could keep
the ceiling up with all she needs. Stacks of canned

yams and white beans, even the kitchen expires
its goods. The oven is a mute, its mouth wired shut.

The house has gone clammy, it sweats and pisses itself.
Wind wraps the maple with plastic bags. Still, the sparrow

hangs in the littered branches. He sings back
to the train whistle trilling along the tracks.

Washing the Saucepans—
The Moon Glows on Her Hands
in the Shallow River

—Kobayashi Issa

It's yet another night when he sits in the yard, wishing the fence
to mend itself, wanting the wily fox to make off

with the chickens. He remembers when they painted the walls
yellow, a box of summer—

when having a house meant something
before talk left the kitchen

and the garden grew thick with vegetables
while the flowerbeds languished.

But the moon loves his dishwasher now more than ever,
her silhouette centered in a square of light.

Her loose hairs curl from the sink steam, lit like fiber optics
around her face: Who needs electricity on a night like this—

when the grass wets his bare feet
and the late-night smokes have lost their thrill.

He swears the stars are smirking. After all,
the moon *is* making love to his wife, holding her hands still.

Conquistadors

His plumage and cocked hat
are a brilliant flag against my former
section of sky. His fingers immersed
to the hilts in my hair, my neck captive
to his other hand, he bows then
when his tongue opens the sealed slit
of my mouth. This is how they cast
their shadows and we spit dirt, we lie
in their darkening. They have built
buildings and ships using the same
strong wrists that can pin and twist,
yet we feed from their hands. I am
kneelingly close to love when he bruises
himself against the sharp complaint
of my hips, and his small ring slivers
a little skin below my eye. His grip
slackens and I part. I resisted forgetting.
I forget resisting. We always bend
our fear into something more useful.

Afternoon with Redón

Odilon, why can't a nymph
learn to love a Cyclops? After all,
we can only focus our two eyes
on the single eye of a lover at any given time.
She would not have to be so shifty;
one to another, the gaze could go unbroken.
His bright blue marble, big as a wheel,
misting over—he'd cry her a lagoon
to bathe in. Why must she just lie there
in molten repose, your damp, vermillion hill
sliding off the canvas? He's got his hungry eye
on her, and he's tragicomic with his clumsy size,
oafish with not knowing right from wrong.
So Galatea may be a mean girl who thrills
with each rejection, but Polyphemus
is like the rest of us with our imperfect
circumspection. Or he's at the very least
like a monster-hearted boy before he buys
his gun, and she's like the heartbreaker,
the boy-teaser, the self-pleaser
who only thought to have some fun.

Riding the Ranch Roads

seems to
have something
to do with the difference
between lonely and lonesome:
lone, the smoke drags in, *some*, the smoke
pours out—two syllables of breathing, tobacco
laden, where the herd dogs sleep with all four paws touching,
where the sun dips down behind a house fixed for dancing, where I hide
my rifle in long grasses, moon-stunned, when dark calls
the rabid from their burrows, where girls hide love
in the folds of their petticoats, where a dinner
bell sends its clang across dusty distances
like a bullet to my windblown
soul or at least it
seems to

Roadside, Railside Diner

Upstate the silver-dollar pancakes
were always made especially
for this little lady
at the diner by the railroad
where the train was always
coming round the mountain
hollering her arrival
and Tootie was always tweaking
my braids pretending
like it wasn't him
his wife always fluttering
like some wheezy bird he'd say to her
don't you have some food to fix
with a wink to my Pop
leaning friendly
against the counter talking
about war he'd gimme
a quarter for an Almond Joy
dropped from the candy machine
with a heavenly thud
and Tootie's brother
went to our church
and had a dog named Barley
who really loved me
but not so much as his master
god forgive him
who had tag sales
and magazines he'd show me
kept mostly in the garage
and if Barley could've talked
I would've asked him
how he could be so loyal
seeing as his master
messed with little girls
and Pop it was maybe good
that you went when you did
cause the diner folded soon after
and the people you trusted
all went a little wrong.

Circus Gravitas

Born to the smell of saw dust
and elephant dung,

I hung like a pendulum
from the bell of the big top,

dangling off a chiffon scarf,
but how long could a veil

resist its gossamer rumor?
How long before flimsiness

rang true? I want to say
that when the knot gave

and the scarf let loose
from the ceiling,

I finally hung on a length of air,
the scarf fluttering and unfurled,

but there was no pause
before the fall. Men in white

strapped me down, clowns
made diversions with trick flowers

and slide whistles. The spectacle
went on with great poofs of make-up

and stroked-up trumpets,
a toothless tiger, and a spangled

strumpet straddling
the lion's unbowed back.

The Hobbyist

A little mesh net will do or
a small pellet shot. The birder

takes her in hand, legs pinched
in his fingers, and gives the neck

a squeeze. From the fluted throat
to belly, he draws his cut. The body

falls from the skin, a persimmon
in sugar, his mouth as roseate

and wet. Her heart is a thimble
of memory. He learns to sew

and stuffs to hide the stitch,
the small bore holes. He uses

the spines for his bottled ships.
Patches of pink at the chest

change to metallic bronze
then green. He keeps them

lined beak to tail. A scarf is a wing
in a magician's case. The skin falls

from the body like a cape
of the disappeared apprentice. He keeps

the skins in catalogued drawers,
vaulted like wives in his cellar floor.

Caught

Swift hunter who am I
the fair lass of slim waist
and blackbird hair or the deer
caught aquiver in the glimmer of your
knife put your hand here and feel my cervine
heart beat will you box it as a present to your queen
or let it flourish wild in the deep forest air
it trembles with danger give me a
head start it's a brambled
path to safety.

II

Where
does cold come from
O scarecrow?

—Kobayashi Issa

Between Rest Stops

We scrawl our miles
on the road's dotted line, through
the flaxen fields, a pageant
of blondes in crushed velvet,
toward the east with the sun in rearview,
half tucked in under the horizon's blanket,
past discarded truck treads,
in the blood spray of mangled deer,
beneath the uniform blue, beside
windmills like hardened men working
the fields with one eye on heaven
and the other on the lonesome horses,
among all the lonesome drivers, where
the rotted barn doesn't fall for lack of trying,
where yellow butterflies are razored onto
our truck's grill and the road
before us always shimmers and
the road behind us holds
the golden hour in a shard
of mirror.

The Lost Boys

It is always telegraphed
when boys are fed
to the elements, so you read
of the one fed first to air
then water from the lip
of a bridge. The one fed
to the fire collected
in the furnace of his
father's sedan. And what
of earth? Old news, the one
searched for with picks
and shovels in the dirt floor
of a basement. I learn
the latest one flung in Oregon
was labeled like mine. In Latin
spectrum means apparition,
and that ghost arcs
from the metal rail over and over
and leaves a trail like a gray
rainbow to the river
below. My own son's
element is water, too.
How he could stand
at the sink and let the wet
feel wash through his fingers
until California is bled dry.
This other boy's mother
must have thought
him cursed by his disorder
or what I call the weird magic
my boy tries to control
and hold in his hands
like a rising lake.

An Oral History of Bodie, California

The mind of the body is optimistic,
even as the pioneer shovels dirt
into the hole, the never ceasing gust
gritting her mouth and eyes, her stillborn
tamped down in the hills pocked
with mines once ribboned in gold.
Even as she thinks to lie down and die,
every morning she rises and wipes
the night's windswept-in silt from the stove,
puts on the kettle, and goes on. In autumn
the draft blasts down the chimney
and scatters sparks across the floorboards,
a blackbird sings if you want to call it song,
and her doctor makes another house call,
but she endures beyond the mill's machinery
grinding to a halt, the pastor leaving
on the only coach, and winter's short supply
of firewood long enough to birth,
or so he was told, the last boy born
in that moribund town.

Sago Mine, West Virginia

The blast was
a rumble, rock cascade,
stone seal. The cave
was a pinpoint
of un-light, a hole,
whole. The wives
cried. The coal
a black ribbon pinned to
a lapel. The gas
was methane in a shaker,
a drunken slew. The lung
an inky sac that
wrapped a greater body
in a bag. The letters
said goodbye. The miners
pulled a curtain, prayed
a sinner's prayer.
The lamp, a night-light
as each crawled
into sleep. The survivor
made a baker's
dozen: the twelve
no longer there.

Cricket
Chirping
  In a Scarecrow's Belly
—Kobayashi Issa

Charlie Perrsen's feed store sign hangs a notch crooked
as fall does a belly crawl into Plainsville. Here's the clincher:

He'd blow his wad on a plane ticket south but the foal's legs
are spindly. He'd make a set of wings with chicken wire

and crow feathers, but he lacks the tack to work with. Wind
catches the hole of his beer bottle, sings a song of reckoning.

Here's the dickering: He'd empty his pockets for a train ticket
north, but the foal's a pretty filly, his Dusty Rose. And the work

is never done. He re-stuffs the scarecrow when the horizon
halves the sun, after September's heat combs the corn silk.

He chirps back to the crickets, rubbing his legs together
under faded sheets and a sickle moon. A sick ol' moon.

Recipe for an Old Fashioned

Being a PI in a shithole town like Detroit
was like being broke and thirsty
for bourbon and something sweet—
it was like tracking down
my brother's deadbeat father
to a cigar-stinking casino in Jersey—
it was not unlike wearing a trench coat
and having a taste for redheads in silk pajamas—
which was just like getting sucker-punch drunk
after midnight in a bar at the right end of town—
which was nearly like staring up at terraces
on a dim-lit street surrounded by dudes
with hair like the black cording of night—
which is why I pull out my gat
with a pivot and spin, with a prayer after sin—
and it was like the Chinese lanterns
burst into flames, which was like some movie
in black and white making a message out of my life—
which is why my head feels shot, why I can't talk
into the light, why I shouldn't mix bourbon
with bitterness or bitterness
with what's too sweet.

Recipe for a Sidecar

It's Halloween in the Castro,
so drink something a little gay.
Sugar the rim of your cocktail glass,
sweeten the *o*, give the tongue
something to lick. Take me,
weaving my tail through the Dorothies,
the daisy chains of blue gingham
and Totos in baskets, no witch in sight.
Take me, knocking back 4 or 5
in the Lucky 13, pirates *yo-ho-hoing*
until the bar tilts like a wooden ship.
Choose a twist or a wedge. Lock yourself
in the stall until a line forms, a line-up
of pixies, nurses, and slutty redheads
ready to piss themselves. No worries,
pretty kitty. A painted devil in a G-string
will draw your whiskers back on.
She'll un-kink your tail. Meanwhile,
the ninjas spin house music
and your masquerading mechanic
boyfriend won't hold your hair back
anymore, so you heave a couple hairballs
into the gutter before he leaves you.
A toast, a toast! Here's to the hurt
that the cat dragged in.

Celebrity Stalking

The celebrities are at it again. They keep
stalking me for poetry. Just the other day
George Clooney tried to deliver a pizza
so I could sign his broadside, Meryl Streep
crouched in my back yard with a first edition
in hand, Julia Roberts broke into my bathroom
to ask about pentameter, and Charlie Sheen left
twenty-six voicemails asking for *sexstinas*
written in the colloquial language of porn,
but these movie stars think they know the real me
behind the poetry because they read tabloids
in line at the super market that detail
the lurid private lives of poets who take lovers,
get caught without make-up, carry small dogs,
enjoy gay trysts, drink absinthe, and own
many-chambered homes with deep-pile
cream carpets, secret rooms, and libraries
the size of Luxembourg. They couldn't know
that I'm allergic to even numbers and no longer
fluent in filthy words. I'm feeling inflamed
on this spring nocturnal in the City of Angels,
a hundred-watt moon on the rise and songbirds
playing their music well past prime time
like neighbors with no children. No moment,
no poet ever safe from the paparazzi,
so we duck into seedy bars while tourists
mug with our tread-upon stars inlaid
along Hollywood Boulevard.

Killing Time in the Green Room

It wasn't easy how everyone watched her
like a clock really and how she reclined
against the leather couch her legs going on and on
crossing and uncrossing like two hands
dangling down into evening hours much more lovely
than expected and how here was her big chance
to explain how someone had to do her job
which wasn't easy, she said, all that addition
and subtraction, and how she kept ticking her pencil
against a pad with little check marks and I almost
couldn't get close enough to slip my shank between
her slim ribs but I did and how she let out a small *o*
and then all around us how everything
even the small girl with a book of horse stickers
came to a flickering halt.

A Spokesperson Said Thoughts and Prayers Go Out

Out like what? Whispers
in a tin can tied with yarn
a thousand miles long
to the can of a woman, her
ear desperately pressed
to its emptiness? Like a loon's
song transmitted by Morse?
Can you fathom the miles
of murky ocean that whale
must sing through? Did you know
some people believe
all sounds ever made
are still present, hovering
like butterflies? Even, say, the whir
of a copy machine out there
in the ether, sent flying
when the first plane hit? Do you see
voices as monarch wings
wheeling through the sky?
If you shout from the window
of a thousand-foot tower
before you fall, where does
that scrap of voice go? Is it still
falling? You mean go out
like candles snuffed by the wind?
You mean out like empathy
in tiny increments marching
like ants made of sound
across the wires of the world?
Did she just hear an Our Father
whiz past? *I'm sorry, I'm sorry,*
she said. *I think you're
breaking up.*

I Shouldn't Even Write This

When the Iranian man told you
in broken English
how he lived each day
through his cancer to see
the dark eyes of his daughter
I knew those lines wouldn't be mine
but when we slept off the tears
in your bed
with the street humming
through an open window
I thought those lines could be mine
and when you gave your body away
for a geometric fix
and when you nearly died
for your next line
like a poem
aches toward the white
at the end of a page
those metaphors were not mine
but when I trace the webbed scars
that lace your body
and when I
see life lived twice
in the clear green of your eyes
those written lines are almost mine
because when I read anything
that puts a boy near a man
like a boy on tiptoe
at the edge of a deep well
I want to tear the page in two
that put him there
and my love
my love that rage
those words are mine.

Corpse Flower

In memoriam James Foley

They've said that the jihadist
narrator spoke in a West London accent, that
the journalist in orange kneeled on the ground, that
he may have denounced America before
the knife met throat and cut back. I'll never know
beyond what they've said on the radio
as I tune to *Morning Becomes Eclectic*
meaning just music. In San Marino
after four years, the Titan Arum
is about to bloom, but you can call it
a corpse flower. I thought that it would look different,
the flower I mean. More like the enormous meaty
flowers of Borneo and less like a new monk stripping
away his purple robes, though they both
pollinate by flies drawn to the scent. Look
them up online. I won't watch how the event
unfolds, yet I hold in my imagination
his mother's hand hovering above the mouse,
cursor blinking over that play arrow, to say nothing
of its barbed end.

Suckling

Sometimes we forget
we're animals
like the bitch nursing
her young: her head
falls back in pleasure
teats used precisely
for what they were made for
mother lust
like the ache in the gut
when the newborn pulls
his first colostrum
sometimes we don't think
we're animals
like the bitch who swats
the pup to the floor
when the tail chewing
wearies and the pup
lets out a yelp.
Mother's trouble
makes the whelp yelp
when the bitch grabs him hard
bitten by manicured
fingernails pinning him
in a sticky car-seat
under a flustering sun.

Henry Ford Hospital, 1932

Collection Museo Dolores Olmedo Patiño, Mexico City

Each of the six red ribbons reach
from Frida's clot of hair, huge sob,
and blood on the sheets. The first
knots around a steel apparatus as medical
coldness, the second bows around
her pelvis painted whole and unbroken,
the third ties around Diego's purple
orchid left wilting on the floor, the fourth
twines around a perfect uterus, all scarlet
and curved, the fifth wraps around a snail
crawling grayly into view. The dawning
of truth. What art means to me. The sixth
is plugged into the umbilicus of a second
fetus, yet I know she'll lose three
and be left with none. A resonance
so close though I only lost one.

Playa de los Muertos

Palms splay the sun's
rays apart like a roof
of fingers. Your beer sweats.

The bees dip their flinty faces
into a Fanta then drown
in orange effervescence.

This is the Mexican way. Sand
and sea, fine beadwork
in primary colors, *terra cotta*

means baked earth. A slow burn
where the ocean curls and scoops
like a machine. It spits a man

on shore, a medic pumps
his face with a bag, and he is
declared. It's the same

machination that wears
the blade from glass.
On the drive home a cross marks

where another Jesus was killed.
Every curve is marked so.
Tonight we'll try to sleep,

but the sea will throw back the moon
with a tawdry light
that mocks our afternoon.

III

The damp pewter days slip around without warning
and we cross over one year and one year.

—Li-Young Lee

victory

the smallest *v* that this poem
ever lifted its head off the pillow,
put on its filthy slippers, and scuffed
off the doorstep in the first place;
that this poem found its way
on and off the leg of a homing pigeon
locked up for life, his old perch
calling to him; that this poem
ever learned to love; that this poem
was breastfed, is attuned to human
touch; that this poem crawled from
the primordial muck, gills to lungs,
and gasped its fins into feet;
that this poem found you and
disrobes for you and isn't made
to feel cheap. the smallest *v*—
divot on a stone in a dry stream, wake
of the swimming bird, bud vase,
flower's throat, point where
two lives meet.

Many Chambered

Heart, or knot of thrumming
muscle, swallow against the cage,

you flutter and become two.
One bird to keep the rhythm, the other

flies to my throat, beats its wings
against my belfry, becomes metaphor.

And somewhere a balloon clears
the clotted chambers, a man groans

in his sleep, a doctor lifts two birds
from a girl's chest, sets in two more.

O, slick red heart, fist-shaped,
when you panic, you fail,

when you harden your walls,
you close shop, when you leak secrets,

another ship sinks. And somewhere
the swallow breaks its wings,

and somewhere the swallow breaks
through the belfry and sings.

Before the Flood

I love the word *antediluvian*—
its fluid logic, the way it runs off the channel
of my tongue, how it places saints, sinners,
and the occasional short-changer in time
at the anterior of the deluge, and I know
the flood referred to is the one where Noah
was said to have gathered mating pairs
on a wooden boat as big as a stadium,
animals packed in steerage. But what about
our Deep South with its discount levees,
where rusted-out cars and particle-board furniture
became leviathans of the sea? What of water-logged
bibles and empty tea pots bobbing like buoys?
What of the last flash of family silver glinting
like fish as it made its way to the bottom?
Of the marooned dogs barking to the birds
who flew straight ahead, pretending not to notice?
What about our short-changed lost in a swirl
of filthy water, damned for nothing more
than being black and poor?

Submersed

The water was a closet I was locked in.
Walls of silt, particulate door, all the divers

were identical mimes making the sign
for trapped. All the divers went away

when murk insinuated the gray-green
of drowning. Fear tasted like a saltine,

my heart a sonar pinging your distance
from me. I pulled myself along the bottom

where starfish were as big as Volkswagens.
We were ghosts finally, moving in some cold

viscosity I never thought I'd leave. I had
my hoses in a bunch because I couldn't spot you,

couldn't even echolocate you. The masks
hid every one of our eyes. The sand dabs

were pale hands that buried themselves
as I crawled, and divers drifted up like souls

kicking their fins, hands raised to the aurora,
to the water-skin of heaven.

Boy with a Halo at the Farmer's Market

The metal halo was bolted into his skull,
little drills secured the scaffold,
so his bones could rebuild themselves.
How truly graced he must have been
to survive a broken neck. Someday
he'll remember how he had to turn
his whole body, caged, to watch
the fruit vendor polish apples. His hair
will cover the evenly spaced scars.
He'll go to school for architecture,
having learned to appreciate girders.
He'll come to love the gold leaf halos
of medieval art, the flash of The Savior
in cracked oils. He may carry himself
a little gingerly, he may never ride a horse
again, but he'll kiss his wife's neck
in a dark theater, taking leisure, blessing
each vertebra, one lucky break at a time.

Bodies of Water

A man and woman sit in a restaurant.
He runs his pinky around the rim of his glass,
and she fidgets with her salad, picking up
each leaf, shredding it into long thin strips. She says to him:
it doesn't need to be a stranglehold;
it can be a warm bath. He says:
couldn't it be an ocean and she replies:
of course it can be ocean—expansive, all-inclusive.
He sips his water and touches his lips
with his fingers. She rolls the corner
of the tablecloth up, then lets it drop.
I don't want to drown, he says. She says:
you can touch my depths. He repeats:
I don't want to drown. A pause. He says:
you will wash me down like colored glass
tumbled in the intense blue of intense you. She laughs and says:
if you leave, I will be the Dead Sea choked with salt. He says:
if I don't you will smash me against rocks
lining the craggy shores. She says:
if you leave, I will be a dry basin
of an extinct Mediterranean—parched and muted
hues lacking that union of blues. He says:
you're exaggerating. She says:
so are you. He says:
waiter, more water please.

Morning Coffee with Chagall

The bride and groom lift off
as if their feet were filled with helium, a bouquet of peonies
clutched in her hands, lips locked as if they're
inflating each other like elegant balloons, such static
buoyancy in new marriage, caught forever on a ceramic mug,
caught forever before Bella would be plucked away,
before he would walk empty-handed
from that hospital in the Adirondacks. Caught when Chagall
still hovered, snagging valentines in his teeth
as the small-motored planes whizzed by, as glossy-winged birds
nodded their approval of his carmine skies. The ideal moment,
as good as a Grecian urn, before the bride rubs her fingers
raw scrubbing potatoes for dinner, before the groom
sweats through his shirt chopping wood, caught before
dinner talk goes cold and taciturn. Held aloft, alive—
before their feet touch the ground, before dishes
need to be done. Before the cup is drained, rinsed
and shut away in the hot spray of my top-of-the-line
machine, caught flying before the gravity
of domestic routine.

Census

How many Springfields
dot our map? How many
are blown through with winter;
how many fathers with blunt,
red fingers, raw from the heaving
of snow? How many fathers try
to make tender with these hands
through the hair of their children?
How many documents detail
the failure? How many mothers
carry their babies to bed
and place mouths against
sleeping faces or the shadows
of bruises; how many mothers
who can't get close enough?
Who can't figure an equation
of hands, arms and mouth
to demonstrate rapture? How many
homes set the electric grid
humming against early darkness
that drives us indoors where
we shuffle our parts to remember
how to touch awkwardly
what we awkwardly love
when what we love rolls
face and bruise away, pushing
our cold hands away?

Lost in Winter, Revised

In memoriam James Kim

As simple as opening the freezer reminds me
that snow is a blanket of blank assembled star

after miserable star. The stars remind me
that you must have seen planes through the trees

as a sailor adrift thirsts for the water in which he floats.
The water reminds me of how you are triggered

in every cold alpine stream, in every copse
of evergreens. The stream and evergreens

remind me of how you were found. How
you were found reminds me that the mountain

is white as a hospital sheet, dumb
as writer's block. Writer's block reminds me

of why we revise. In my first draft
they found you starved and alive.

Winter Distances

The country road winds
between barren orchards
from one small whistle-stop
to another, and in houses
set back from the road—
where Christmas lights
try to make something
with early darkness—
men smack their wives
but don't mean to, and wives
watch their reflections flicker
in windows facing the woods.
The police roll down
the roads, radios giving
a crackle now and then.
      Between us
the flatlands sit fallow,
snow makes its own angels
when it melts on a pond,
a man puts his face in his hands
at precisely this moment,
and someone is having a tea party
in her trailer. The police roll down
those roads with their radios
turned off. We watch
the same moon rise
at different times.
      Behind your flickering
the big city is a loud puzzling
of sirens and cabs. People
move underground, a lawyer
is having a binge and purge
six doors down, but when
your bourbon cracks its ice,
three hours later, *l'chaim,*
I am your echo. When you curl
in bed for sleep, later my body
takes the same shape.
      Here,
the mountain lion attacks bikers,
the lake barely freezes, then thaws,
and a girl makes a game
of distances.

In Discovery Park

The hummingbird follows me
through the park and it takes a certain
ear to hear her. You say you wish
I lived more in my body. If you call me
      light-boned, I'll try. Grass fields
and stands of trees roll down to the water
in a palette of wheat tones, and the water
is a flat slate of gray that tips up
to the sky, as if the water had pivots
      at each end. You wish I were less
of a looking glass. The coin plants have gone
to seed again. How many could
      I pay you to keep my heart
a little longer? A million silvered discs
pour through your fingers.

School Rules

Your freshly minted kindergartner says,
the fire bell rings and we line-up, and because
you know drills are in place to be ready,
you also know what came before.
Like that turn-of-the-century school,
heavy-wooden rafters and clapboard,
the children climbing the walls
as flames shook their red fists at the sky:
the worst tragedy of its kind, they said.
Welcome to the age of preparedness.
So you pick your boy up from his school
of concrete, ever on lockdown behind
chain-link where the mothers cling,
unable to pass through. Welcome
to a new school made by guns trained
on little kids. In the morning students
gather in the center of a blacktop slab
and sit in groups, then they file into
the barracks. A few small signs—
a tetherball and four-square markings—
tell you this is not a prison, though you know
the edifice is about what is kept out
instead of in. Welcome to the new way
we learn. Still, as you detangle your fingers
from the fence, your boy lost in the fray,
you can't help think how easy it would be
to prop a rifle in the hard crux of a steel
diamond and aim at children squirming
in their uniforms. How you can never
really be safe from random madness.
Welcome to the way you think now.

Kicked Around

The ball was too chubby and pink to think "kick it!"
so I was last in kickball and first in oddball. Now I'm
a full-grown waitress expecting more than these grease stains
crisscrossing my mother's day t-shirt at mother's day brunch
as I balance the plates up my arms like a circus act,
a failed kickballer who thought tenderness should count
for something. So what if this poem were a rubber school ball
aimed at the head of the woman who gave me the stink-eye
and no tip? What if I carried hash like purple mountains majesty
topped with a little fluff of poached egg? She said her food was cold
so I blamed it on the toast. The kitchen tried I tried to tell her,
but it didn't matter. She would have kicked me if she could.
Fuck that bitch. She's no better than me: a waitress
who spins hash and eggs into poetry.

Correct Me

Darling correct me
if I'm wrong and please
pin me to the page
with a graphite
spike O beloved proof-
reader put your
sharp lines
through me break
the spine of my best
book cross me off
with that flourishing
squiggle take my voice
down a notch my sub-
jugator my conjugator
make a mockery
of me use your
scarlet cudgel a
dildo a stiletto
heel in the face of my
fever my
which and that
feel dirty turn it
over to your soft pink
and rub me rub me
until my cleanest white
comes through.

Twice-Missed Carriage

The headache
is like a spike
through the skull's
base in back
where the neck
meets it and up
and around
the inside like
a misshapen
metal girder, the
headache set off
by heavy blood
flow much further
below, heavier
than the normal
drops from my
monthly clock,
the hope-dump
headache set
off by a sip too
many meant to
wash away in
the most figurative
way the shed
ovum, what might
have been. The
headache set off
by loss's glance
back, its
double
take.

The Emperor

Is terrible
in his monster shirt
half-carried, half-dragged
through the doors. His fit
makes heads swivel
while I pin serenity
to my forehead as we aim
for my hack. He can't
uncrack my smile
with his screaming.
At the dining table
his lunch lavished before him
he tries to hit his servant
over nothing more than
a red train, red-faced with
tears, kicking and squawking
because the emperor
was made to put it away.
Carried off to his room
his feast on hold
bars on his bed thank god
because he's an animal now
for two more roars
then a dumb thumb-
sucking silence.
Behold now how
his excellence sleeps.

A Vision in Stride Rite

The boy throws his sandal
over the edge of the pram
his other leg bent not quite ninety
just enough to drape the hand
that clutches the bunch
of champagne grapes
as he surveys his subjects
plucks fruit to mouth
while the palm fronds wave
in the late California afternoon.
Purple stains are dropped blossoms
on a cartoon shirt pulled across
a belly in repose. Here he is,
Baby Bacchus, making the most
of privilege as his servant
puts her shoulder to the wheel
and shoves on
up the hill.

Passing the Barnyard Graveyard

I sang Elvis to the shorn sheep,
and they didn't run away.
I sang Patsy to the fine ass
who chewed crabgrass and brayed.
I sang Bonnie to the bunny:
mini, milk-eyed, and gray.
I sang Johnny to the billy goat.
He could have listened all day.
I sang Piaf to the gravestones:
Fantômes, parlez vous Français?

About the Author

Sonia Greenfield was born and raised in Peekskill, New York, and earned an MFA from the University of Washington and an MPW from the University of Southern California. Author of poetry chapbook *Circus Gravitas* (2014) and two-time Pushcart Prize nominee, her poems, essays, and fiction have appeared widely, including in *2010 Best American Poetry*, *The Antioch Review*, *The Bellevue Literary Review*, *Cimarron Review*, *Cream City Review*, *The Massachusetts Review*, *Meridian*, and *Rattle*. She lives with her husband and son in Los Angeles, California, where she teaches writing at USC.